I Am a Butte

A Story About Big, Beautiful Changes

Story and Photographs by Sally Stone

wisdom
heart
Wisdom Heart Publications

A special thank you to Dr. Lincoln P. Brower for his
expert advice on the scientific content of this book.

*—Dr. Brower is the Distinguished Service Professor of Zoology Emeritus at the
University of Florida, Research Professor of Biology at Sweet Briar College, and
author/co-author of more than 200 publications on the monarch butterfly*

To get free downloads, free book offers, and art prints visit:
www.NaturesHealingImages.com

Attention Schools & Businesses:

For information on bulk purchases for educational, business, or promotional use, contact the author through NaturesHealingImages.com or DrSallyStone.com.

Photo Credits

Photography by Sally Stone

Photo Equipment: Canon Rebel xSi, Canon 7D, Canon 100-400L, Canon 100mmL

Locations: Chicago Botanic Garden; Techny Prairie, Northbrook, IL; Peggy Notebaert Nature Museum, Chicago, IL; South Texas Botanical Gardens and Nature Center, Corpus Christi, TX; and the author's backyard

Butterfly illustrations, emergent caterpillar, and monarch emerging from chrysalis via Shutterstock

Monarch egg photo via Pixnio

Dear Readers: All internet addresses were active and appropriate at the time of publication. The publisher has no control over and assumes no liability for the material or links on those websites.

ISBN: 978-0-9969159-3-9 (paperback)
ISBN: 978-0-9969159-4-6 (ebook)

For my mom,
who taught me to be still in nature
and watch for the magic.

For nature—you are beautiful,
good, and full of wonder.

wisdom
heart

Wisdom Heart Publications

I am a butterfly.

At first I didn't know I was a butterfly.

You know why?

Because I wasn't.

I was just a teeny-tiny egg on a leaf.

I sat there for a few days.

Then I hatched.

But I still wasn't a butterfly.

Now I was a caterpillar—
a squishy caterpillar
with no wings
at all
whatsoever.

I munched leaves and
grew to be a big caterpillar.

Then something
really strange happened.

I turned into this!

I still wasn't a butterfly, obviously.

And I wasn't a caterpillar anymore.

Nope.

Now I was a *chrysalis*.

Inside my chrysalis, it was really dark.

I was scared at first.

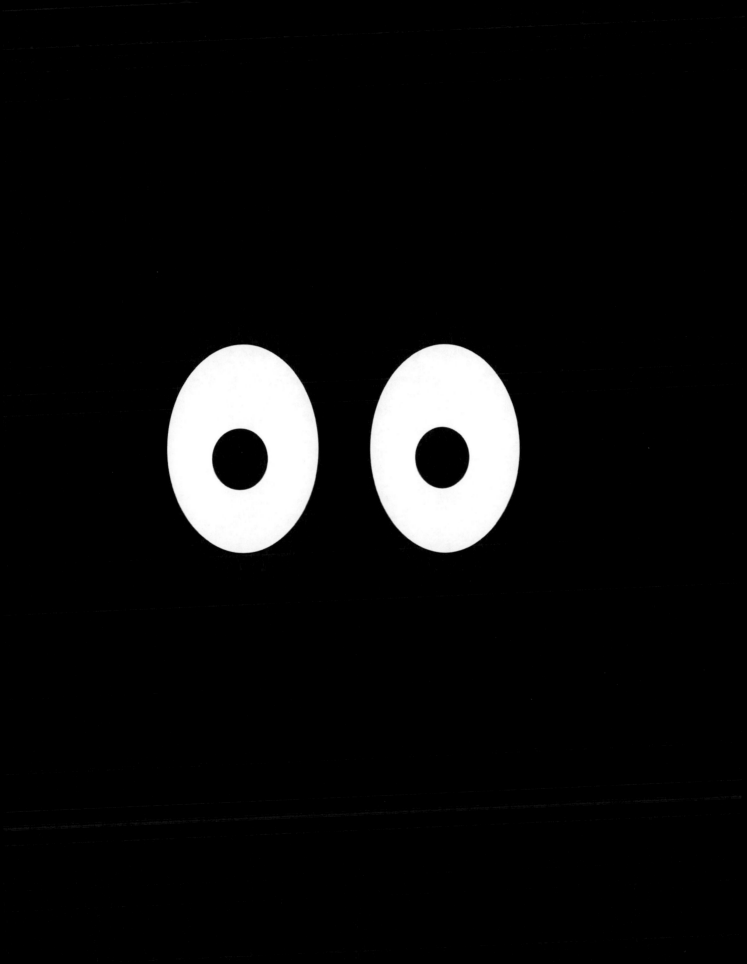

But then I relaxed
in the soft, velvety darkness.

I could feel myself changing.

Then one day, light came
streaming through my chrysalis!

I started to move.

I stretched and I pushed
and I pulled.

But I couldn't crawl like a
caterpillar anymore.

Something REALLY BIG
had changed!

I had wings!

I was a butterfly!

I liked it.

I perched on a flower to dry
my new wings in the sunshine.

The warm sun felt good.

I used my wings to fly to all the flowers.

My new tongue was like a straw.

I used it to sip sweet flower nectar!

When I was a caterpillar,
I liked eating leaves.

But now I like nectar even more.

Now that I'm a butterfly,
I have lots of new butterfly friends.

They come in all different
sizes, shapes, and colors.

People try to catch us and
touch our shimmering wings.

My wings are fragile,
so I always fly away!

But if you're quiet and still, one of us
might land on your sleeve...

...or tickle your fingers with our tiny feet.

Soon I will lay eggs on
this milkweed plant.

They will go through big,
beautiful changes
just like me.

I am a butterfly.

And I like it!

Who are you?

Facts About Butterflies

1. Butterflies glue their eggs to leaves.

2. Monarchs lay eggs only on milkweed plants.

3. Monarch caterpillars eat only milkweed leaves.

4. A monarch caterpillar turns into a chrysalis as it sheds its skin.

5. Monarchs born in the summer live for a few weeks.

6. Monarchs born in the fall migrate and overwinter in parts of Mexico and southern California.

7. Groups of butterflies are called "flutters."

8. Butterflies taste with their feet.

9. Most butterflies feed on flower nectar.

10. Butterflies drink nectar with their proboscis.

11. Butterflies stand in puddles to drink minerals.

12. The big change from caterpillar to butterfly is called "metamorphosis."

If you wear bright colors, butterflies might think you're a flower and land on you.

Without change, there'd
be no butterflies.

The Monarch Butterfly Life Cycle

Monarchs change into butterflies more quickly in hot weather, and more slowly in cooler weather.

I am an egg for three to five days.

I am a caterpillar for about two weeks.

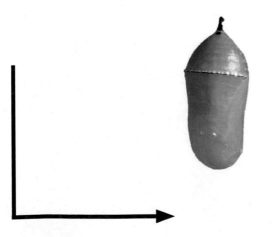

I am a chrysalis for about one week.

Now I lay eggs.
My life cycle
begins again.

When my chrysalis looks
clear, I move out fast. It
takes just a few minutes!

Please meet more of my beautiful butterfly friends!

Are Monarchs Endangered?

Monarch butterflies are disappearing.
They are at risk of becoming endangered.
Here's how you can help:

1. Monarchs lay eggs only on milkweed plants because that's what monarch caterpillars eat. You can plant milkweed in your own yard to give monarchs a place to lay eggs, eat leaves, drink nectar, and just hang out.

   Visit this website to find out which types of milkweed grow best in your area: www.nwf.org/Garden-For-Wildlife/About/Native-Plants/Milkweed.aspx

2. When you plant flowers in your yard or in pots, monarchs can drink their nectar.

   Visit this website to find out which flowers monarchs like best: www.nwf.org/Garden-For-Wildlife/About/Native-Plants/Monarch-Nectar-Guides.aspx

Monarch Resources

Read research and support monarchs with a donation.
monarchconservation.org/
www.worldwildlife.org/species/monarch-butterfly

Read more monarch facts from National Geographic.
www.nationalgeographic.com/animals/invertebrates/m/
monarch-butterfly/

Raise your own monarchs at home or at school.
monarchbutterflygarden.net/
www.monarchwatch.org/

Watch a monarch caterpillar turn into a chrysalis!
https://youtu.be/G8hQU-Zj99g

Learn More

Topics of interest on monarchs and butterflies:

- Monarch migration

- Monarch endangerment

- Visit a butterfly garden
  www.butterflywebsite.com/gardens/

- Ways to protect monarchs and other butterflies
  www.biologicaldiversity.org
  www.monarchwatch.org/

These monarchs visited the author's garden while she wrote this book!

If you plant milkweed, and other nectar flowers, monarch butterflies may visit your garden, too.

About the Author

Sally Stone is an author, photographer, certified hypnotist, and certified health coach. Her love for nature inspired her to learn photography so she could spend more time connecting to its magic. Her photos have won several awards including Audubon's Top 100 and a Chicago Botanic Garden Special Mention.

When Sally isn't writing, taking pictures, or coaching, you can find her taking long walks in nature, watching birds, talking to trees, and smelling the flowers. She also loves to pet everyone's dogs, meditate, work in her native garden, drink herbal tea, go to the movies, hang out at the beach, and spend time with loved ones.

Sally's love for children's books began in childhood and never ended. For 23 years she worked with children and teachers, first in her classroom, then as a coach and university professor. She's helped hundreds of children write their own stories. Sally earned her master's degree and doctorate in education from National-Louis University and has won two teaching awards.

To get free prints, sign up for free books, and see more butterflies and nature photos visit Sally's website: NaturesHealingImages.com

Join Sally's Facebook Community, Nature's Healing Images: facebook.com/healingimages11/

Follow Sally on Instagram: instagram.com/drsallystone11/

Other Books by Sally Stone

Golden Words Book Awards
2017 Readers' Favorite Silver Medal
2016 Indie Human Relations Gold Medal
2016 Nautilus Silver Medal
2015 IPPY Silver Medal
2015 IIN Launch Your Dream Book Top Ten

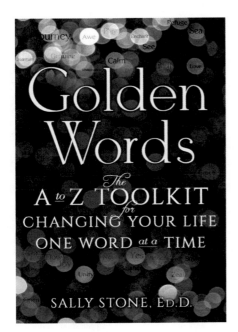

"Words are spells." And what a powerful collection of spells this book is! With practical, interactive guidance on how to use them—integrated with full mind, body, and soul health and well-being. Move over Harry Potter —there's a new wizard in town! *Amazon Review*

For more information, visit Sally's Amazon Author Page or her website DrSallyStone.com.

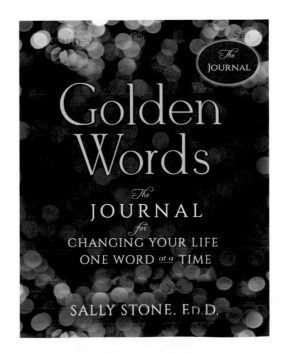

Made in the USA
Middletown, DE
01 March 2023

25982552R00031